W9-BYI-804

DRAW cars

by Doug DuBosque

REDFORD TWP, PUBLIC LIBRARY

PEEL productions, inc.

APR 0 9 2007

For my brother Rick, who encouraged
my car enthusiasm at an early age.

*(Without revealing how to work the
clutch on his Triumph TR-4)*

Copyright ©1993, 1998 Douglas C. DuBosque. All rights reserved, including
the right of reproduction in whole or in part, in any form.
Published by Peel Productions, Inc.
Manufactured in the United States of America

Cataloging-in-Publication Data

DuBosque, D. C.
       Draw Cars / by Doug DuBosque
              p.   cm.
       Summary: provides step-by-step instructions for drawing popular cars,
including racing cars, exotics, and off-road vehicles.
       ISBN 0-939217-29-5 (pbk)
       1. Automobiles in art--Juvenile literature. 2. Drawing--technique--
Juvenile literature. [1. Automobiles in art. 2. Drawing--Technique.] I.
Title.
NC825.A8D83 1997
743'.89629222--dc21
                                                                97-25458

Distributed to the trade and art
markets in North America by

NORTH LIGHT BOOKS,
an imprint of F&W Publications, Inc.
4700 East Galbraith Road
Cincinnati, OH 45236

(800) 289-0963

DRAW cars

Contents

Supplies...

Find a **comfortable place to draw** – with decent light, so you can see what you're doing.

As you start to learn about car designs, shapes and proportions, don't worry too much about materials.

Use a **pencil that's longer than your finger.**

Sharpen your pencil when it gets dull!

Get a **separate eraser.** My favorite is a *kneaded* type, available in art supply and craft stores (the eraser on your pencil will disappear quickly).

For smooth shading with a soft pencil, consider a **tortillon, or blending tool.**

For practice drawings, use **recycled paper** – for example, draw on the back of old photocopies or computer printouts.

Always **draw lightly at first**, so you can erase problems as you need to.

Save your drawings and learn from them.

Enjoy drawing *great* cars!

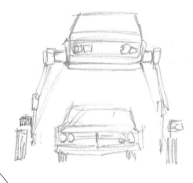

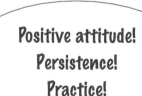

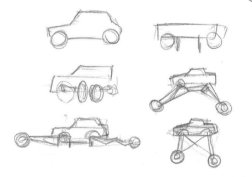

Part One

Draw a car from the side

In the next *few pages,* you'll look closely at the basic body parts and lines that shape a car. You'll learn how to get proportions and details just right. Pay close attention!

Do this chapter first!

(Really!)

Dodge Stratus

*Before you start, look carefully at your **reference material**.*

For this drawing, your reference material will be this finished drawing (my reference material for this drawing was a magazine advertisement.)

Start with a light horizontal line for the ground.

The Ground.

Carefully draw a circle for the wheel.

A Wheel. Don't worry if it isn't perfectly round at first.

Always ask yourself: how many wheels (or wheel *diameters*) would fit between the front and back wheel?

You won't see many cars where the answer is two.

Nor will you see many cars where the answer is seven!

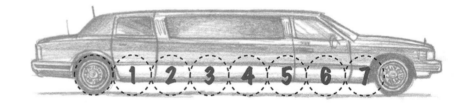

On the Stratus, the front and rear wheel are separated by about 3½ diameters, which is typical of many cars.

Always start out *lightly!*

Carefully measure the distance between the wheels, then draw a light circle for the second wheel.

Look again at your *reference material.* Lightly draw the line at the bottom of the windows. Observe its height above the wheels, and notice how it slopes slightly down to the front.

Look again at your *reference material.* Find the top of the roof. Lightly draw this line.

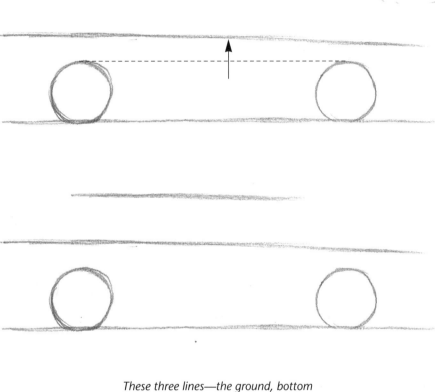

*These three lines—the ground, bottom of window, and roof—are **basic lines** you'll need to draw **any** car.*

The details can be a little complicated at the front and rear end of the car. For now, just make a light vertical line to mark the front of the car, with another line cutting back to the wheel.

Look again at your *reference material* to see where to end the car. Make a light vertical line there, then another cutting forward to the wheel.

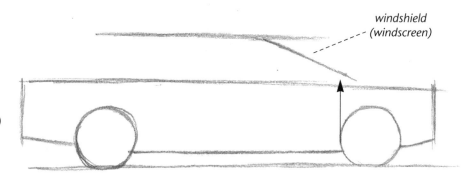

Look at the windshield. How far forward does it extend, compared to the back of the front wheel? *(This varies from car to car.)* Lightly sketch the windshield line.

windshield (windscreen)

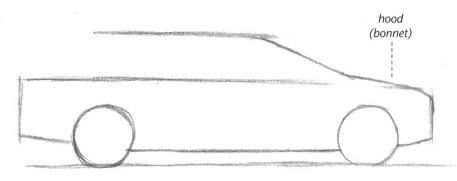

Add the line, joining the bottom of the windshield and carrying forward, with a slight curve.

hood (bonnet)

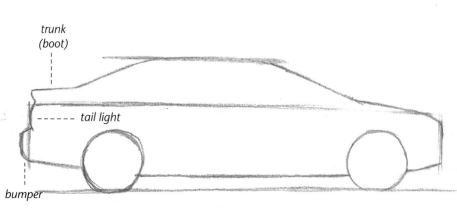

Notice how the rear window and trunk are higher than the hood. Draw them. Now take another look at your *reference material*, and add the curves of the bumper and tail light.

trunk (boot)

tail light

bumper

Always start out *lightly!*

Extremely

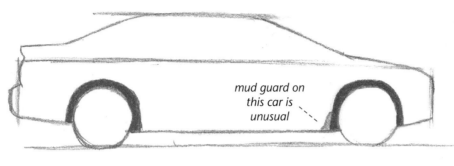

mud guard on this car is unusual

important…draw the dark cut-out portion of the body that surrounds the wheels. These dark *wheel wells* are key to making your car drawing look real!

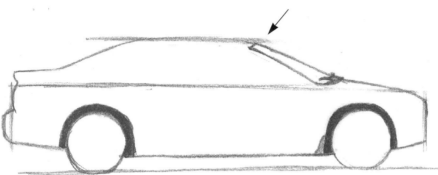

Add the side and top windshield lines (notice the angle at the top of the windshield). Draw windshield wipers.

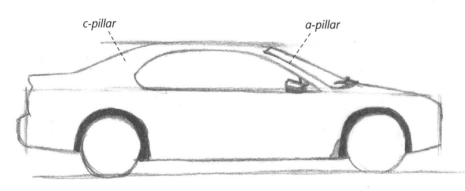

c-pillar

a-pillar

The outline of the side windows contributes much to the car's style. Draw the outline of the side windows. By drawing this shape, you've also drawn the A- and C-pillars. Add the mirror.

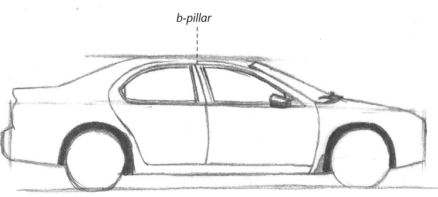

b-pillar

Look carefully at the size of the doors. Typically, on a four-door *sedan,* the front doors are bigger (a *coupe* has two doors). Outline the doors, windows and b-pillar (draw the door seam through the middle of it).

Why do chicken coops have two doors?

(Because if they had four doors, they'd be chicken sedans.)

Draw the rear window.

Add the tail light, and the body seam.

Outline and curve the front end. *(Ooops...I had to change mine to make it stick out a bit more.)* Draw bumper and light details.

Always look for horizontal lines on the sides of cars. Designers add them to make cars look sleeker.

Draw the trim extending along the side.

Always start out *lightly!*

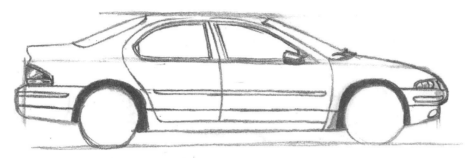

Add another horizontal line, above the bottom of the doors, and extending to the rear end of the car.

Draw door handles. Erase guidelines you no longer need.

highlights

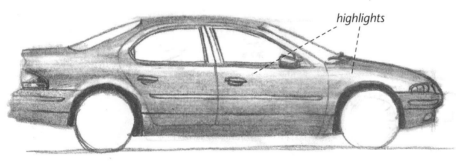

Look carefully at the *reference material,* and add shading to your drawing. You might smooth it, as I did, with a *tortillon* or blending tool (see page 4). Then you can use your eraser to add highlights. Spend as much time as you need at this stage.

Turn your drawing as you draw to avoid smudging it with your hand.

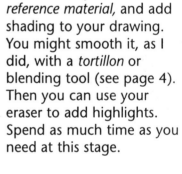

Now sharpen your pencil and go over details and lines, making them as crisp as you can.

All done!

...just kidding!

Notice those *round things* the car sits on. They have two parts: the *wheel* and the *tire.* Draw a smaller circle in each tire for the real wheel.

Having trouble drawing circles? See page 61 to learn how to draw them perfectly!

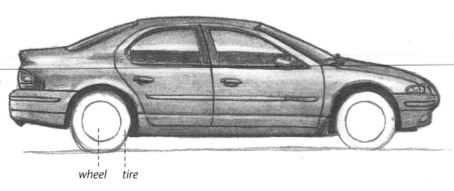

wheel   tire

Darken the tires. For best effect, leave a little highlight at the top of the top, and the top of the bottom.

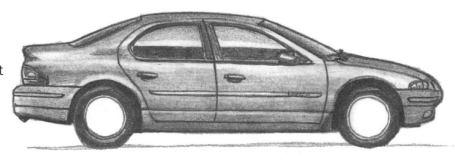

Draw the pattern of the wheels.

Add details to the wheels, and shading.

All done!

(Really!)

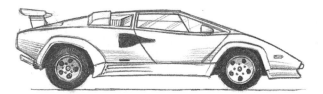

Part Two

More cars in profile

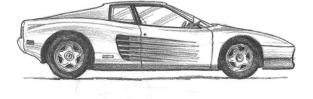

In the next few pages you will use the final drawing as your reference material. Look carefully at the finished drawing, then follow a few easy steps to add the lines, shapes and details you see.

Outrageous!

None of the cars pictured here have step by step instructions in this book. But, with these drawings as reference material, and your positive attitude, persistence and practice...

...you'll be drawing outrageous cars in no time!

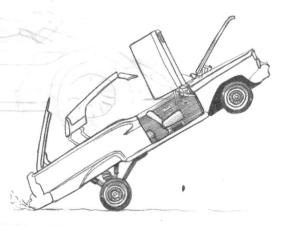

Audi Avus

*Before you start, look carefully at your **reference material** (for now, my finished drawing).*

Draw the ground line. Using the wheel diagram above, draw the wheels the correct distance apart. Draw the basic body lines.

Complete the overall shape of the car.

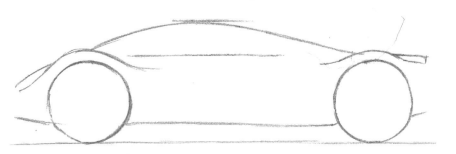

Add:
- front and rear bumpers
- windows
- wheel wells
- lights
- rear view mirror
- tires and wheels

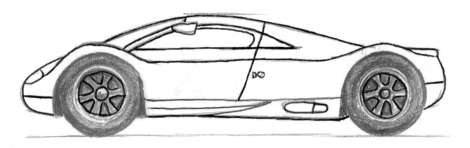

Draw other details you see (or want—hey, it's your drawing!). Add shading.

Remember:
- *Start out lightly!*
- *Turn your drawing as you work. Use a piece of scrap paper to keep your hand off finished parts.*
- *While your pencil is sharp, go over fine details and make lines cleaner. As it gets duller, add shading.*
- *Clean up any smudges with your eraser. Make sure all final lines are crisp and sharp.*

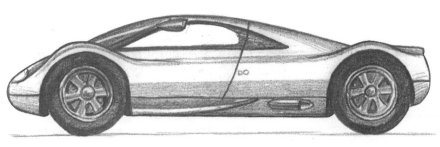

Vector W12

*Before you start, look carefully at your **reference material** (for now, my finished drawing).*

Draw the ground line. Using the wheel diagram above, draw the wheels the correct distance apart. Draw the basic body lines.

Complete the overall shape of the car.

Add:
- windows
- air scoops
- wheel wells
- lights
- rear view mirror
- fuel cap
- tires and wheels

Draw other details you see (or want—hey, it's your drawing!). Add shading.

Remember:
- *Start out lightly!*
- *Turn your drawing as you work. Use a piece of scrap paper to keep your hand off finished parts.*
- *While your pencil is sharp, go over fine details and make lines cleaner. As it gets duller, add shading.*
- *Clean up any smudges with your eraser. Make sure all final lines are crisp and sharp.*

Ferrari F50

Before you start, look carefully at your reference material (for now, my finished drawing).

Draw the ground line. Using the wheel diagram above, draw the wheels the correct distance apart. Draw the bottom body line, the distinctive slanting center line, and the front and rear bumper lines.

Add the line for fenders and spoiler, which curves down to the bumper. Draw the windshield and engine cover. Reshape the rear bumper.

Add:
• wheel wells
• tail lights
• side air scoop
• rear view mirror

Draw other details you see (or want—hey, it's your drawing!). Add shading.

Remember:
• *Start out lightly!*
• *Turn your drawing as you work. Use a piece of scrap paper to keep your hand off finished parts.*
• *While your pencil is sharp, go over fine details and make lines cleaner. As it gets duller, add shading.*
• *Clean up any smudges with your eraser. Make sure all final lines are crisp and sharp.*

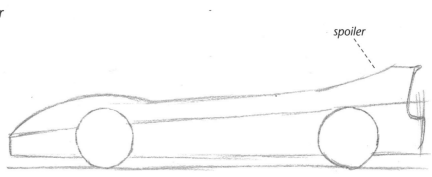

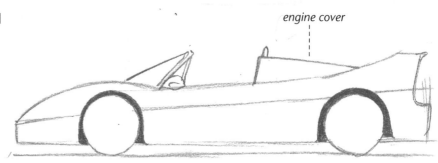
spoiler

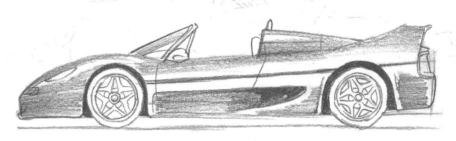
engine cover

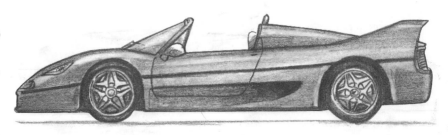

Always start out *lightly!*

*Before you start, look carefully at your **reference material** (for now, my finished drawing).*

Draw the ground line. Using the wheel diagram above, draw the wheels the correct distance apart. Draw the basic body lines.

Complete the overall shape of the car.

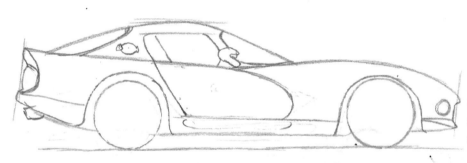

Add:
- windows
- pillars A and B
- wheel wells
- side body seams
- radical side vent
- lights
- rear view mirror
- fuel cap

Draw other details you see (or want—hey, it's your drawing!). Add shading.

Remember:
- *Start out lightly!*
- *Turn your drawing as you work. Use a piece of scrap paper to keep your hand off finished parts.*
- *While your pencil is sharp, go over fine details and make lines cleaner. As it gets duller, add shading.*
- *Clean up any smudges with your eraser. Make sure all final lines are crisp and sharp.*

Shelby Cobra

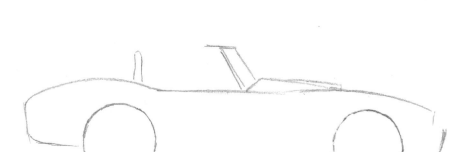

*Before you start, look carefully at your **reference material** (for now, my finished drawing).*

Draw the ground line. Using the wheel diagram above, draw the wheels the correct distance apart. Draw the basic body lines.

Complete the overall shape of the car.

Add:
- windshield
- roll bar
- wheel wells
- side exhaust, vents
- lights
- rear view mirror

Draw other details you see (or want—hey, it's *your* drawing!). Add shading.

Remember:
- *Start out lightly!*
- *Turn your drawing as you work. Use a piece of scrap paper to keep your hand off finished parts.*
- *While your pencil is sharp, go over fine details and make lines cleaner. As it gets duller, add shading.*
- *Clean up any smudges with your eraser. Make sure all final lines are crisp and sharp.*

Corvette

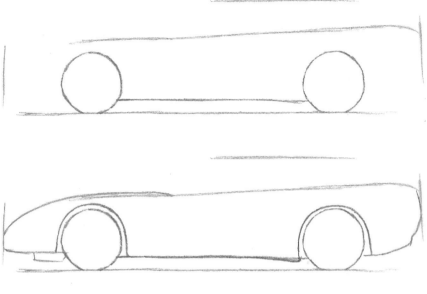

*Before you start, look carefully at your **reference material** (for now, my finished drawing).*

Draw the ground line. Using the wheel diagram above, draw the wheels the correct distance apart. Draw the basic body lines.

Complete the overall shape of the car.

Add:
- windows
- pillars A and B
- wheel wells
- side vent
- side lights
- rear view mirror
- fuel cap

Draw other details you see (or want—hey, it's *your* drawing!). Erase guide lines. Add shading.

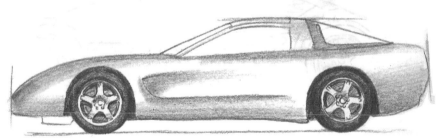

Remember:
- *Start out lightly!*
- *Turn your drawing as you work. Use a piece of scrap paper to keep your hand off finished parts.*
- *While your pencil is sharp, go over fine details and make lines cleaner. As it gets duller, add shading.*
- *Clean up any smudges with your eraser. Make sure all final lines are crisp and sharp.*

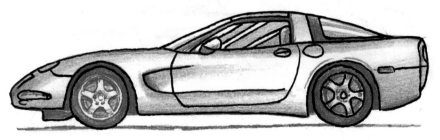

BMW 318

*Before you start, look carefully at your **reference material** (for now, my finished drawing).*

Draw the ground line. Using the wheel diagram above, draw the wheels the correct distance apart. Draw the basic body lines.

Complete the overall shape of the car.

Add:
- windows
- split rear window
- pillars A, B, and C
- wheel wells
- side trim
- lights
- rear view mirror
- steering wheel

Draw other details you see (or want—hey, it's *your* drawing!). Add shading.

Remember:
- *Start out lightly!*
- *Turn your drawing as you work. Use a piece of scrap paper to keep your hand off finished parts.*
- *While your pencil is sharp, go over fine details and make lines cleaner. As it gets duller, add shading.*
- *Clean up any smudges with your eraser. Make sure all final lines are crisp and sharp.*

Always start out *lightly!*

*Before you start, look carefully at your **reference material** (for now, my finished drawing).*

Draw the ground line. Using the wheel diagram above, draw the wheels the correct distance apart. Draw the basic body lines.

Complete the overall shape of the car.

Add:
- windows
- four window pillars
- wheel wells
- side trim
- lights
- rear view mirror
- fuel cap
- luggage rack

Draw other details you see (or want—hey, it's *your* drawing!). Add shading.

Remember:
- *Start out lightly!*
- *Turn your drawing as you work. Use a piece of scrap paper to keep your hand off finished parts.*
- *While your pencil is sharp, go over fine details and make lines cleaner. As it gets duller, add shading.*
- *Clean up any smudges with your eraser. Make sure all final lines are crisp and sharp.*

Lamborghini Diablo Roadster

*Before you start, look carefully at your **reference material** (for now, my finished drawing).*

Draw the ground line. Using the wheel diagram above, draw the wheels the correct distance apart. Draw the basic body lines. Look carefully—they're unusual!

Complete the overall shape of the car.

Add:
- wheel wells
- side scoops
- running lights
- rear view mirror

Draw other details you see (or want—hey, it's *your* drawing!). Add shading.

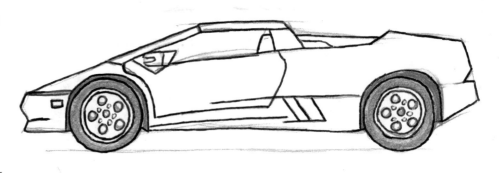

Remember:
- *Start out lightly!*
- *Turn your drawing as you work. Use a piece of scrap paper to keep your hand off finished parts.*

This little number costs more than many people's houses—a lot more. There's not much cargo room (!), so if you did own one of these, you'd probably drive it a lot. For example, grocery shopping: you'd need one trip for milk, another for bread, another for vegetables....

Volkswagen Beetle

*Before you start, look carefully at your **reference material** (for now, my finished drawing).*

Draw the ground line. Using the wheel diagram above, draw the wheels the correct distance apart. Draw the basic body lines.

Complete the overall shape of the car, starting with the distinctive window shape.

Add:
- wheel wells
- blacked-out b-pillar
- door handle
- lights
- rear view mirror

Draw other details you see (or want—hey, it's *your* drawing!). Add shading.

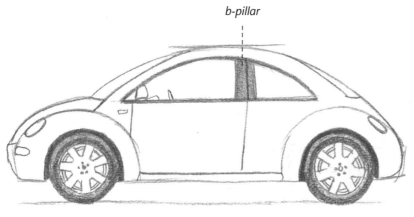

b-pillar

Remember:
- *Start out lightly!*
- *Turn your drawing as you work. Use a piece of scrap paper to keep your hand off finished parts.*
- *While your pencil is sharp, go over fine details and make lines cleaner. As it gets duller, add shading.*

The one millionth VW beetle was built 'way back in 1955 (see page 58). Unlike the old beetle, this new design has the engine in front.

1906 Franklin

Before you start, look carefully at your **reference material** (for now, my finished drawing).

Draw the ground line. Using the wheel diagram above, draw the wheels the correct distance apart. Draw the basic body lines.

Complete the overall shape of the car.

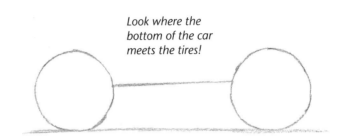

Look where the bottom of the car meets the tires!

Add:
- windows
- pillars A, B, and C
- fenders
- side trim
- wheel spokes
- head light, side lantern
- rear view mirror*

Look where the front and rear meet the tires!

Draw other details you see (or want—hey, it's *your* drawing!). Add shading.

Remember:
- *Start out lightly!*
- *Turn your drawing as you work. Use a piece of scrap paper to keep your hand off finished parts.*
- *While your pencil is sharp, go over fine details and make lines cleaner. As it gets duller, add shading.*
- *Clean up any smudges with your eraser. Make sure all final lines are crisp and sharp.*

*I-don't-think-soooo…

Always start out *lightly!*

1934 Ford Model A

Before you start, look carefully at your **reference material** *(for now, my finished drawing).*

Draw the ground line. Using the wheel diagram above, draw the wheels the correct distance apart. Notice where the bottom of the car meets the tires! Draw the basic body lines.

Complete the overall shape of the car. Notice where the front and rear meet the tires!

Add:
- windows
- pillars A, B, and C
- fenders
- side vents
- lights
- rumble seat
- bumpers
- spare tire

rumble seat

Draw other details you see (or want—hey, it's *your* drawing!). Add shading.

Remember:
- *Start out lightly!*
- *Turn your drawing as you work. Use a piece of scrap paper to keep your hand off finished parts.*
- *While your pencil is sharp, go over fine details and make lines cleaner. As it gets duller, add shading.*
- *Clean up any smudges with your eraser. Make sure all final lines are crisp and sharp.*

1946 Chrysler Town and Country

*Before you start, look carefully at your **reference material** (for now, my finished drawing).*

Draw the ground line. Using the wheel diagram above, draw the wheels the correct distance apart. Draw the basic body lines.

Complete the overall shape of the car.

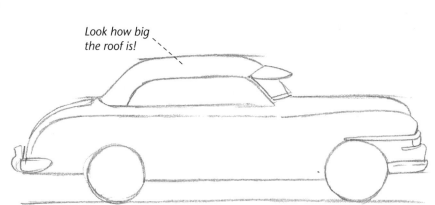

Look how big the roof is!

Add:
- windows
- pillars A, B, and C
- wheel wells, fenders
- side paneling
- lights
- rear view mirror
- luggage rack
- hood ornament

Draw other details you see (or want—hey, it's *your* drawing!). Add shading.

Remember:
- *Start out lightly!*
- *Turn your drawing as you work. Use a piece of scrap paper to keep your hand off finished parts.*
- *While your pencil is sharp, go over fine details and make lines cleaner. As it gets duller, add shading.*

Always start out *lightly!*

1961 Corvette

Before you start, look carefully at your **reference material** *(for now, my finished drawing).*

Draw the ground line. Using the wheel diagram above, draw the wheels the correct distance apart. Draw the basic body lines.

Complete the overall shape of the car.

Add:
* wheel wells
* side trim
* (useless) bumpers
* door handles

Draw other details you see (or want—hey, it's *your* drawing!). Add shading.

Curved windshield—you don't see this on newer cars

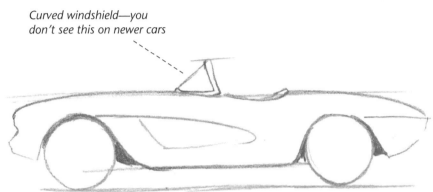

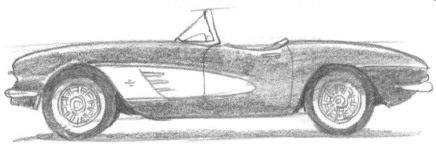

Remember:
* *Start out lightly!*
* *Turn your drawing as you work. Use a piece of scrap paper to keep your hand off finished parts.*
* *While your pencil is sharp, go over fine details and make lines cleaner. As it gets duller, add shading.*
* *Clean up any smudges with your eraser. Make sure all final lines are crisp and sharp.*

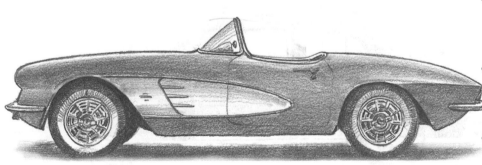

1956 Chevy

*Before you start, look carefully at your **reference material** (for now, my finished drawing).*

Draw the ground line. Using the wheel diagram above, draw the wheels the correct distance apart. Draw the basic body lines.

Complete the overall shape of the car.

Note the angle

Add:
- windows
- pillars A, B, and C
- wheel wells
- side trim
- rear view mirror
- hood ornament

Draw other details you see (or want—hey, it's your drawing!). Add shading.

Remember:
- *Start out lightly!*
- *Turn your drawing as you work. Use a piece of scrap paper to keep your hand off finished parts.*
- *While your pencil is sharp, go over fine details and make lines cleaner. As it gets duller, add shading.*
- *Clean up any smudges with your eraser. Make sure all final lines are crisp and sharp.*

Always start out *lightly!*

*Before you start, look carefully at your **reference material** (for now, my finished drawing).*

Draw the ground line. Using the wheel diagram above, draw the wheels the correct distance apart. Draw the basic body lines.

Complete the overall shape of the car.

Add:
- windows
- pillars A, B, and C
- wheel wells
- side trim
- fin with tail light
- rear view mirror
- windshield wipers
- door handle

Draw other details you see (or want—hey, it's *your* drawing!). Add shading.

(Invent a character to drive this gas-guzzling monster!)

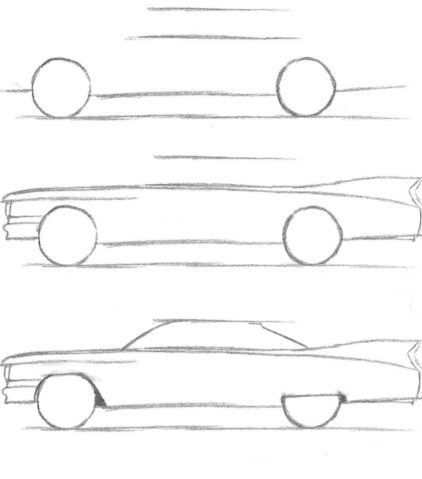
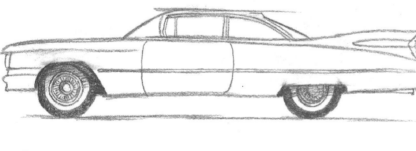
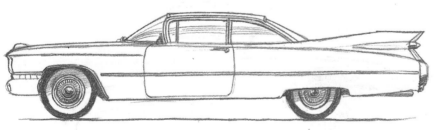

Remember:
- *Start out lightly!*
- *Turn your drawing as you work. Use a piece of scrap paper to keep your hand off finished parts.*
- *While your pencil is sharp, go over fine details and make lines cleaner. As it gets duller, add shading.*
- *Clean up any smudges with your eraser. Make sure all final lines are crisp and sharp.*

Land Rover

*Before you start, look carefully at your **reference material** (for now, my finished drawing).*

Draw the ground line. Using the wheel diagram above, draw the wheels the correct distance apart. Draw the basic body lines.

Complete the overall shape of the car. Notice where the bottom of the car meets the tires.

Add:
- windows
- pillars A, B, and C
- wheel wells
- side trim
- lights
- spare tire, mud flaps
- luggage rack

Draw other details you see (or want—hey, it's *your* drawing!). Add shading.

Remember:
- *Start out lightly!*
- *Turn your drawing as you work. Use a piece of scrap paper to keep your hand off finished parts.*
- *While your pencil is sharp, go over fine details and make lines cleaner. As it gets duller, add shading.*
- *Clean up any smudges with your eraser. Make sure all final lines are crisp and sharp.*

Hummer

Before you start, look carefully at your reference material (for now, my finished drawing).

Draw the ground line. Using the wheel diagram above, draw the wheels the correct distance apart.

Draw the basic body lines. Notice where the bottom of the car meets the tires!

Complete the overall shape of the car.

Add:
- windows
- pillars A, B, and C
- wheel wells
- side details
- lights
- fuel caps

Draw other details you see (or want—hey, it's *your* drawing!). Add shading.

Remember:
- *Start out lightly!*
- *Turn your drawing as you work. Use a piece of scrap paper to keep your hand off finished parts.*
- *While your pencil is sharp, go over fine details and make lines cleaner. As it gets duller, add shading.*
- *Clean up any smudges with your eraser. Make sure all final lines are crisp and sharp.*
- *When you see it coming, this vehicle has the right of way.*

Uncle Bill's Ratty Old Pickup

*Before you start, look carefully at your **reference material** (for now, my finished drawing).*

Draw the ground line. Using the wheel diagram above, draw the wheels the correct distance apart. Draw the basic body lines.

Complete the overall shape of the wreck.

Add:
- windows
- wheel wells
- side trim
- door handle
- exhaust system

Draw other details you see (or want—hey, it's *your* drawing!). Add shading.

Remember:
- *Start out lightly!*
- *Turn your drawing as you work. Use a piece of scrap paper to keep your hand off finished parts. Uncle Bill will be grateful.*
- *While your pencil is sharp, go over fine details and make lines cleaner. As it gets duller, add shading.*

Uncle Bill thinks of this ratty, clunky, smoking old pickup truck as family. Which it is, sort of. Unfortunately.

Always start out *lightly!*

But think of the possibilities!

If…Uncle Bill takes it into the garage, gets out his welding torch, chops and channels it, adds some aircraft hydraulics… suddenly it's a screaming lowrider street rod!

Or maybe he installs a few dozen extra shock absorbers, raises the whole thing so high you need a stepladder to get in, then drops in an engine like something from Cape Canaveral.

Then again, maybe Uncle Bill's going to light up a quarter mile drag strip with a nitro-burning funny car so powerful it needs extra wheels behind to keep it from flipping over backward!

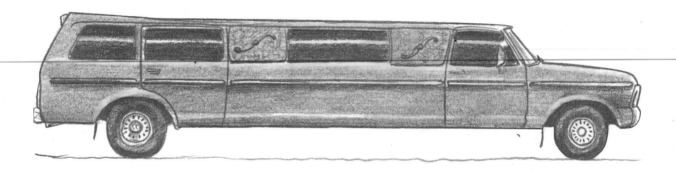

It may turn out that Uncle Bill is a very practical sort, saving to turn his ratty ol' pickup into a classy limo…

…then again, perhaps he lives a secret life as a undercover defender of democracy. He just wants you to think it's a ratty ol' pickup, when in fact it's a high-tech Scud-buster!

Perhaps you don't have an Uncle Bill.

(Do you have a bus driver?)

Part Three

Draw a car from an angle

In the *next few pages, you'll look closely at a car from an angle. You'll learn how to draw the basic body parts and lines that shape the car—step by step.*

Dodge Stratus (again!)

Drawing a car from an angle is more complicated than drawing it from the side. Always use *reference material*.

For this drawing, your reference material will be this finished drawing (my reference material for this drawing was a magazine advertisement.)

When you draw a car from an angle, the ground line will usually be at an angle. Draw the ground line.

Notice how perspective makes the rear wheel smaller than the front.

Draw ovals (ellipses) for the wheels. Take care to space them properly.

Add the line of the bottom of the car.

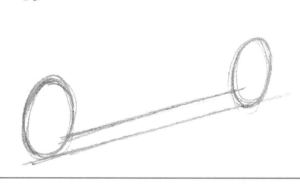

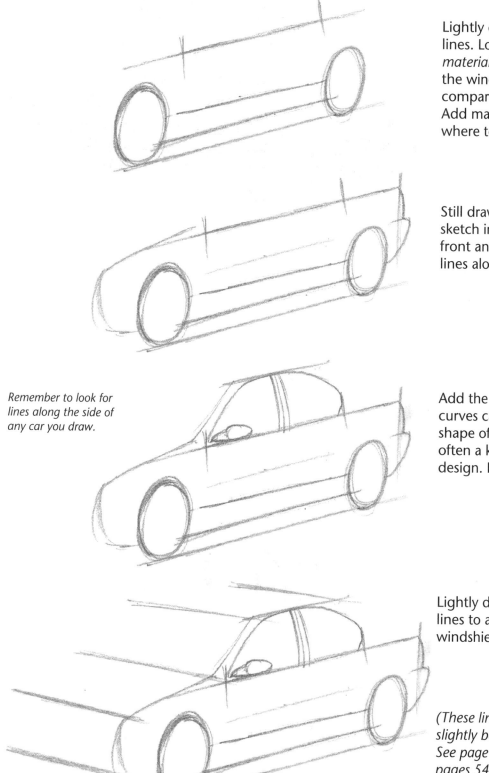

Lightly draw the basic body lines. Look at your *reference material* and observe where the window pillars lie, compared to the wheels. Add marks to show yourself where to draw them.

Still drawing very lightly, sketch in the shapes of the front and rear. Add the trim lines along the side.

Remember to look for lines along the side of any car you draw.

Add the windows. Draw the curves carefully, since the shape of the windows is often a key part of the car's design. Draw the mirror.

Lightly draw parallel guide lines to add depth to roof, windshield, and front.

(These lines may converge slightly because of perspective. See page 40; also T-Bucket on pages 54-55 shows extremely "wide-angle" perspective).

Draw a curved line to form the contour of the roof and the windshield.

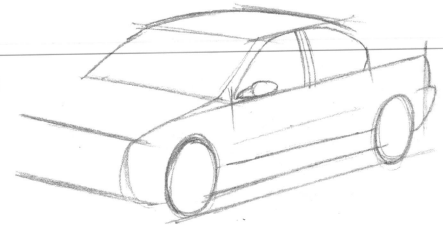

Look carefully at your *reference material,* and draw guide lines to form the front.

You may be able to draw the front without first drawing guide lines. I find, though, that it's easy to get it wrong without the guide—especially when the front curves, as it does here.

Add the rear deck and C-pillar.

C-pillar

Draw headlights and other details. Erase guide lines you no longer need.

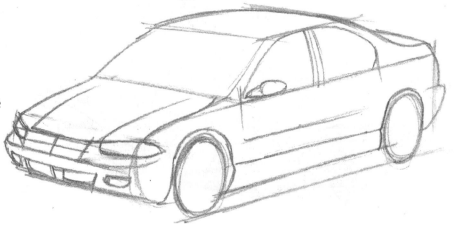

Always start out *lightly!*

Look for light and dark areas in your *reference material.* (Generally, the wheel wells are the darkest part.)

Using a soft pencil, add shading.

If you have a tortillon (see page 4) for blending, you can use it (you can also use a small wad of paper or even your finger to make the shading smoother).

With a sharp pencil (HB is better than 2B or 3B), carefully draw the details of the wheels. Turn your paper to make it easier. Put scrap paper between your hand and the drawing to avoid smudging it.

To finish, go over all lines with a sharp pencil (preferably HB), and add any remaining details: door seams, handles, windshield wipers, headlight details….

Don't forget the cast shadow!

All done!
Super Stratus!

About Perspective

Perspective comes into play every time you draw a car from an angle.

Sometimes—as in the case of this 1959 Cadillac—the effects are very noticeable. If you draw the basic body lines, you'll see they extend back to a single *vanishing point.**

The wide-angle lens on the camera makes this photograph more dynamic.

Here you can see a Mercedes-Benz sport utility vehicle with a similar "wide-angle" view. This customized vehicle appeared in a certain dinosaur movie. Because of the dramatic wide-angle view, it looks as though it's ready to leap into action, perhaps chasing a *Pachycephalosaurus.***

The basic lines converge (get closer together) as they go toward the background.

With a telephoto lens, this advertising photo gives a different impression: the vehicle looks much less wild.

(Which is probably just as well; most people don't buy cars to chase dinosaurs.)

* for more on perspective, see *Learn To Draw 3-D*

** for more on Pachycephalosaurus, see *Draw Dinosaurs*

Part Four

Draw more cars from an angle

In the next few pages, you'll look at different cars from different angles. Following the basic approach laid out in Part Three, explore their similarities and differences, in design and form, and in the viewpoints from which you see them.

Surprise!

The cars pictured here don't appear in Part Four! Use them as reference material, and you can draw them using what you learned in Part Three.

BMW Z3

*Before you start, look carefully at your **reference material** (for now, my finished drawing).*

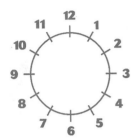

What are the angles formed by the wheels, on the side, and—if you could see them—the two front wheels? Compare these basic angles with the clock face if you need to. Pay special attention to perspective: how much do the lines converge toward the background? How much smaller is the rear wheel?

Draw the side ground line and the wheels. Add the basic body lines.

Draw lines to show depth, on the rear deck, front, and windshield. Look at the clock face if you find the angles confusing. Add the distinctive curves of the hood.

With all these lines in place, add more details.

Always start out *lightly!*

Finishing the drawing takes the most effort, so make sure you're happy with your drawing so far.

Look at it in a mirror, or hold it up to the light and look at it through the back of the paper. Does everything look correct, forward and backward? If not, what can you fix to make the drawing look better? Start over if you need to.

When you're satisfied with the angles and proportions, add more details. Add details while your pencil is sharp.

Add shading when your pencil is dull. If you have more than one pencil, use a softer one (3B) for shading and a harder one (HB) for details.

Look again at the final drawing. Add any details you've missed.

Remember:
- *Start out lightly!*
- *Turn your drawing as you work. Use a piece of scrap paper to keep your hand off finished parts.*
- *While your pencil is sharp, go over fine details and make lines cleaner. As it gets duller, add shading.*
- *Clean up any smudges with your eraser. Make sure all final lines are crisp and sharp.*

Stand back and admire your creation!

Ruf CTR-2

*Before you start, look carefully at your **reference material** (for now, my finished drawing).*

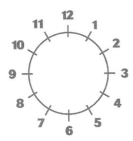

What are the angles formed by the wheels, on the side, and—if you could see them—the two front wheels? Compare these basic angles with the clock face if you need to. Pay special attention to perspective: how much do the lines converge toward the background? How much smaller is the rear wheel?

Draw the ground line, the wheels and the bottom body line.

Draw guide lines for adding depth. Notice how they converge toward a distant vanishing point, because of perspective.

Add curved lines for the fender and roof. Draw the other headlight, the window pillars and the rear view mirror.

When is a Porsche not a Porsche? When it's a Ruf, so completely altered that it actually has a new serial number. Built with a Porsche body shell, this Ruf costs slightly more than a Lamborghini Diablo Roadster. It goes from 0-60 MPH in 3.6 seconds. Which is fast.

***Extremely** fast.*

Always start out *lightly!*

Finishing the drawing takes the most effort, so make sure you're happy with your drawing so far.

Look at it in a mirror, or hold it up to the light and look at it through the back of the paper. Does everything look correct, forward and backward? If not, what can you fix to make the drawing look better? Start over if you need to.

When you're satisfied with the angles and proportions, add more details. Add details while your pencil is sharp.

Add shading when your pencil is dull. If you have more than one pencil, use a softer one (3B) for shading and a harder one (HB) for details.

Look again at the final drawing. Add any details you've missed.

Remember:
- *Start out lightly!*
- *Turn your drawing as you work. Use a piece of scrap paper to keep your hand off finished parts.*
- *While your pencil is sharp, go over fine details and make lines cleaner. As it gets duller, add shading.*
- *Clean up any smudges with your eraser. Make sure all final lines are crisp and sharp.*

Stand back and admire your creation!

Dodge Durango

*Before you start, look carefully at your **reference material** (for now, my finished drawing).*

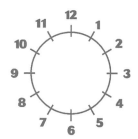

What angles are formed by the wheels, on the side and in the front? Compare these basic angles with the clock face if you need to. Pay special attention to perspective: how much do the lines converge toward the background? How much smaller is the rear wheel?

Draw the ground line, the wheels and the basic body lines.

Draw lines showing depth on the front of the car and windshield. Again, look at the clock face if you find the angles confusing.

Add the curves of the hood, then carefully draw the curves of the front grill and headlights. Observe the amount of clearance in the wheel wells. Draw these. Add the bottom of door lines.

Always start out *lightly!*

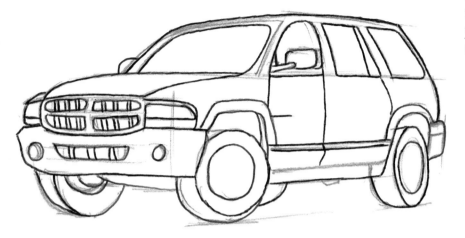

Finishing the drawing takes the most effort, so make sure you're happy with your drawing so far.

Look at it in a mirror, or hold it up to the light and look at it through the back of the paper. Does everything look correct, forward and backward? If not, what can you fix to make the drawing look better? Start over if you need to.

When you're satisfied with the angles and proportions, add more details. Add details while your pencil is sharp.

Add shading when your pencil is dull. If you have more than one pencil, use a softer one (3B) for shading and a harder one (HB) for details.

Look again at the final drawing. Add any details you've missed.

Remember:
- *Start out lightly!*
- *Turn your drawing as you work. Use a piece of scrap paper to keep your hand off finished parts.*
- *While your pencil is sharp, go over fine details and make lines cleaner. As it gets duller, add shading.*
- *Clean up any smudges with your eraser. Make sure all final lines are crisp and sharp.*

Stand back and admire your creation!

Plymouth Prowler

*Before you start, look carefully at your **reference material** (for now, my finished drawing).*

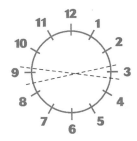

What are the angles formed by the wheels on the side, and in the front? Compare these basic angles with the clock face if you need to. Pay special attention to perspective: how much do the lines converge toward the background? How much smaller is the rear wheel?

Draw the ground line, the wheels and the basic body lines.

Draw the curved lines that form the pointed front of the car. Add the windshield and back body line. Again, look at the clock face if you find the angles confusing.

Add the other front wheel, the two-part bumper and fenders.

Always start out *lightly!*

Finishing the drawing takes the most effort, so make sure you're happy with your drawing so far.

Look at it in a mirror, or hold it up to the light and look at it through the back of the paper. Does everything look correct, forward and backward? If not, what can you fix to make the drawing look better? Start over if you need to.

When you're satisfied with the angles and proportions, add more details. Add details while your pencil is sharp.

Add shading when your pencil is dull. If you have more than one pencil, use a softer one (3B) for shading and a harder one (HB) for details.

Look again at the final drawing. Add any details you've missed.

Remember:

- *Start out lightly!*
- *Turn your drawing as you work. Use a piece of scrap paper to keep your hand off finished parts.*
- *While your pencil is sharp, go over fine details and make lines cleaner. As it gets duller, add shading.*
- *Clean up any smudges with your eraser. Make sure all final lines are crisp and sharp.*

Stand back and admire your creation!

Formula 1 Racer

*Before you start, look carefully at your **reference material** (for now, my finished drawing).*

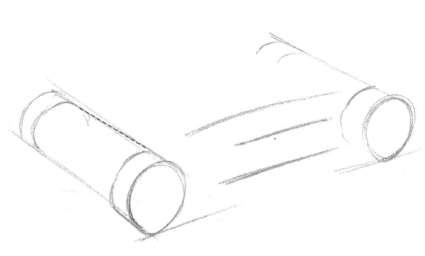

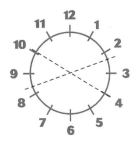

What angles do the wheels form, on one side, and between the two front wheels? Compare these basic angles with the clock face if you need to. Pay special attention to perspective: how much do the lines converge toward the background? How much smaller is the rear wheel?

Draw the ground lines, the wheels, the basic body lines, and in this case the top of the air scoop.

Draw depth guide lines to find the correct placement of the other wheels. Again, look at the clock face if you find the angles confusing.

Add the rounded point of the front of the car, the rim of the cockpit, and the cowling that covers the engine.

cowling

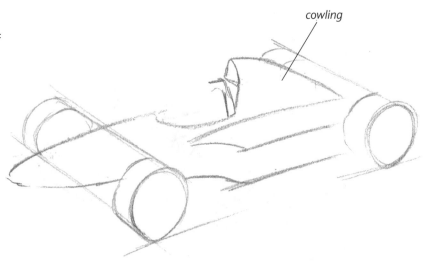

Always start out *lightly!*

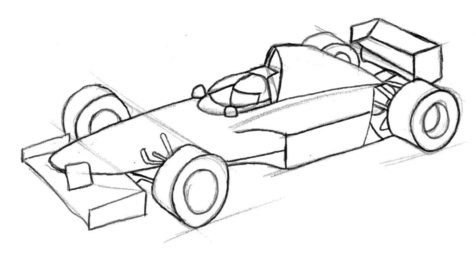

Finishing the drawing takes the most effort, so make sure you're happy with your drawing so far.

Look at it in a mirror, or hold it up to the light and look at it through the back of the paper. Does everything look correct, forward and backward? If not, what can you fix to make the drawing look better? Start over if you need to.

When you're satisfied with the angles and proportions, add more details. Add details while your pencil is sharp.

Add shading when your pencil is dull. If you have more than one pencil, use a softer one (3B) for shading and a harder one (HB) for details.

Look again at the final drawing. Add any details you've missed.

Remember:
- *Start out lightly!*
- *Turn your drawing as you work. Use a piece of scrap paper to keep your hand off finished parts.*
- *While your pencil is sharp, go over fine details and make lines cleaner. As it gets duller, add shading.*
- *Clean up any smudges with your eraser. Make sure all final lines are crisp and sharp.*

Stand back and admire your creation!

1957 Chevy

*Before you start, look carefully at your **reference material** (for now, my finished drawing).*

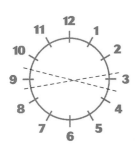

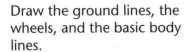

What angles are formed between the wheels on the side, and—if you could see it—between the two front wheels? Compare these basic angles with the clock face if you need to. Pay special attention to perspective: how much do the lines converge toward the background? How much smaller is the rear wheel?

Draw the ground lines, the wheels, and the basic body lines.

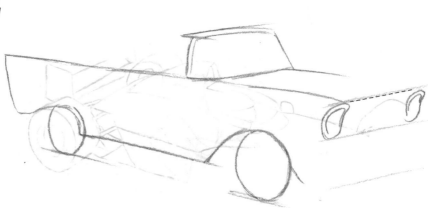

Draw lines showing depth on the front of the car and windshield. Look at the clock face if you find the angles confusing. Add the distinctive headlights, rear end line and flaring wheel wells.

Add the curves of the windshield, side trim, front bumper, and other details you see.

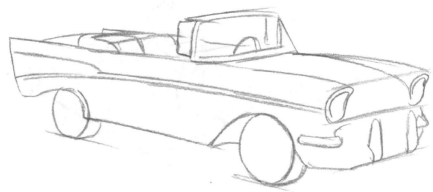

Always start out *lightly!*

Finishing the drawing takes the most effort, so make sure you're happy with your drawing so far.

Look at it in a mirror, or hold it up to the light and look at it through the back of the paper. Does everything look correct, forward and backward? If not, what can you fix to make the drawing look better? Start over if you need to.

When you're satisfied with the angles and proportions, add more details. Add details while your pencil is sharp.

Add shading when your pencil is dull. If you have more than one pencil, use a softer one (3B) for shading and a harder one (HB) for details.

Look again at the final drawing. Add any details you've missed.

Remember:

- *Start out lightly!*
- *Turn your drawing as you work. Use a piece of scrap paper to keep your hand off finished parts.*
- *While your pencil is sharp, go over fine details and make lines cleaner. As it gets duller, add shading.*
- *Clean up any smudges with your eraser. Make sure all final lines are crisp and sharp.*

Stand back and admire your creation!

T Bucket Street Rod

*Before you start, look carefully at your **reference material** (for now, my finished drawing).*

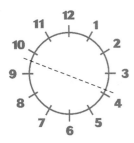

What are the angles formed by the wheels, on one side, and by the two front wheels? Compare these basic angles with the clock face if you need to. Pay special attention to perspective: how much do the lines converge toward the background?

Compare basic body lines with the clock face to be sure they run at the correct angle.

Draw the side wheels, and the basic body lines.

Draw lines for the windshield, and to show depth on the side, front, and top of the car. Draw guide lines to find the correct placement of the other front wheel. Add additional ellipses to add depth to the wheels.

Always start out *lightly!*

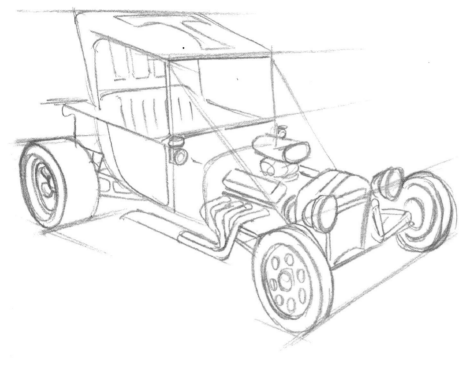

Finishing the drawing takes the most effort, so make sure you're happy with your drawing so far.

Look at it in a mirror, or hold it up to the light and look at it through the back of the paper. Does everything look correct, forward and backward? If not, what can you fix to make the drawing look better? Start over if you need to.

When you're satisfied with the angles and proportions, add more details. Add details while your pencil is sharp.

Add shading when your pencil is dull. If you have more than one pencil, use a softer one (3B) for shading and a harder one (HB) for details.

Look again at the final drawing. Add any details you've missed.

Remember:
- *Start out lightly!*
- *Turn your drawing as you work. Use a piece of scrap paper to keep your hand off finished parts.*
- *While your pencil is sharp, go over fine details and make lines cleaner. As it gets duller, add shading.*
- *Clean up any smudges with your eraser. Make sure all final lines are crisp and sharp.*

Stand back and admire your creation!

Funny Car

*Before you start, look carefully at your **reference material** (for now, my finished drawing).*

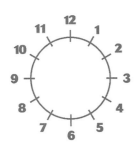

What angles are formed by the wheels, on one side, and by the two front wheels? In this case, almost none. Because this viewpoint is almost at ground level, the lines go practically straight out to the side (and all the wheels appear at the same level as well). Look at how big that rear wheel is!

Draw the ground line and the wheels.

Notice how the bottom of the car lines up with the bottom of the front wheel, but the middle of the rear wheel? Draw the body lines.

Add depth lines on the front of the car and windshield.

Draw the fenders overlapping the wheels.

A funny car is designed to race on a 1/4-mile drag strip. Its engine may produce 5,000 horsepower. In the short time it runs, it consumes 15 gallons of nitromethane fuel at $18 per gallon.

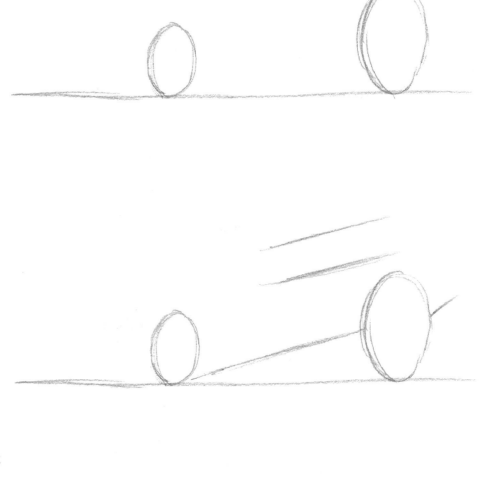

Always start out *lightly!*

Funny Car

Finishing the drawing takes the most effort, so make sure you're happy with your drawing so far.

Look at it in a mirror, or hold it up to the light and look at it through the back of the paper. Does everything look correct, forward and backward? If not, what can you fix to make the drawing look better? Start over if you need to.

When you're satisfied with the angles and proportions, add more details. Add details while your pencil is sharp.

Add shading when your pencil is dull. If you have more than one pencil, use a softer one (3B) for shading and a harder one (HB) for details.

Look again at the final drawing. Add any details you've missed.

Remember:
- *Start out lightly!*
- *Turn your drawing as you work. Use a piece of scrap paper to keep your hand off finished parts.*
- *While your pencil is sharp, go over fine details and make lines cleaner. As it gets duller, add shading.*
- *Clean up any smudges with your eraser. Make sure all final lines are crisp and sharp.*

Stand back and admire your creation!

The rear spoiler is made of aluminum and magnesium and capable of producing 5,000 pounds of downward force on the rear tires.

The rear "slicks" are 18 inches wide, nearly ten feet in circumference, and inflated with only four pounds pressure!

The Gallery

Here's a weird collection of vehicles to give you ideas. Try drawing them!

A. *Ford Model T - 1920s.*

B. *1933 Ford Model Y - British (note mirror on right side)*

C. *1950s dream car, designed to resemble jet aircraft.*

D. *1,000,000th Volkswagen "Beetle" rolled off the assembly line in 1955*

E. *Exotic car called Isdera from an unusual angle, showing the slope of its side windows and size of its windshield.*

A

B

C

D

E

Always start out *lightly!*

F

G

F. A concept car called the Ethos, shown at a car show in the hope of selling the design to a car manufacturer.

G A prototype (huge!) minivan that I don't think ever made it into production…

H. Lamborghini Countache – compressed perspective from photo (on the side of a model box!) taken with a telephoto lens.

I. Landrover from a similar angle – interesting comparison to the Lamborghini!

J. Mazda racing prototype. I used to own one of these…

H

I

…just kidding!

J

Tips and Tricks: Some Basics

Use reference material: find pictures in magazines or books when you can't look at actual cars. Look at details, light and dark areas, and the effects of perspective from the camera angle.

Turn your paper as you draw to take advantage of the point of your pencil, and the natural way your hand draws curves.

Put scrap paper under your hand to keep from smearing parts of the drawing you've already finished.

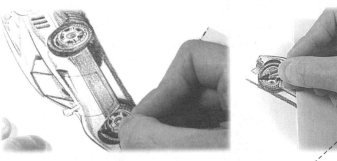

Protective paper keeps drawing clean

Kneadable eraser can be pinched into a point for close work

Use your eraser to create highlights and to clean up any smudged areas.

Use different pencils. Pencils range from 6B (softest and darkest) to 9H (hardest). A normal 2B pencil works well for sketching and shading, but a harder HB makes crisper lines – I even use a 5H, which is very hard, for very fine details.

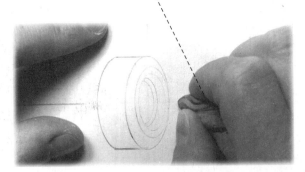

For very smooth shading, use a soft pencil and a *tortillon* (see page 4), a wound-up paper stick made for blending pastels.

Tips and Tricks: Making Wheels Round

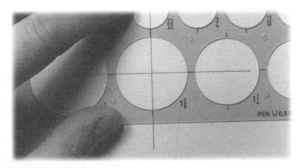

"Aren't wheels always round?" you ask. No, in fact, they're only round when you look at them in exactly the right way. Otherwise they're elliptical (see next page). Round wheels can be both fun and frustrating to draw.

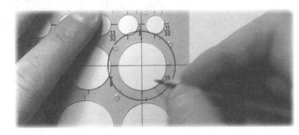

If you want perfect circles, you might want to try a transparent circle template. Make a horizontal and vertical line, then align them with the marks on the template. Then draw circle after circle, using different size holes in the template.

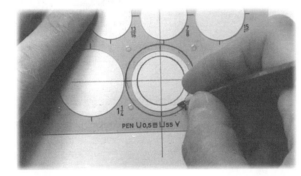

When you start looking at wheel (or hub cap) designs, you'll find a bewildering variety. Most are divided into five spokes or holes. But some have four, some have six, some have none, some have seven, or nine, or eleven, or...well, *count them for yourself!*

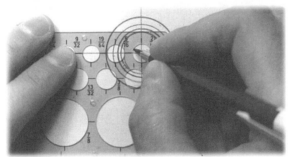

The more you look, the more you'll see. Have fun hunting for and drawing cool wheels!

Tips and Tricks: Wheels from an Angle

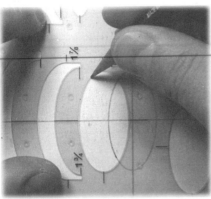

Although I have a template for ellipses, I don't use it. I prefer to draw freehand.

These photos show how the ellipses go together to make a wheel from an angle.

Starting with a horizontal and vertical line, draw one ellipse. Next, slide the template along the horizontal line, and draw part of a second ellipse, the same size as the first.

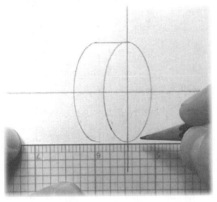

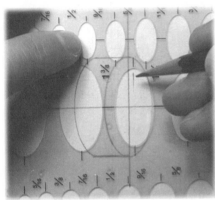

Use a ruler to connect them to make the top and bottom of the tire. Now slide the template to the right, slightly beyond the first vertical line, and make a smaller ellipse.

Though you don't have to, you can add another, still smaller ellipse on the same vertical axis. Then slide the template left to the first vertical line for the rim of the wheel.

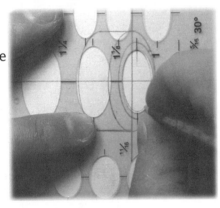

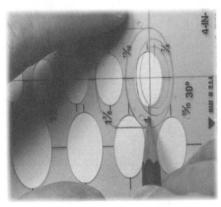

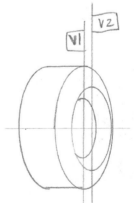

V1=vertical axis used for largest and smallest ellipse

V2=vertical axis used for smallest ellipse

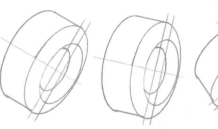

When viewing wheels from above, rotate the axes. Note that they remain perpendicular to each other.

Tips and Tricks: Imagination!

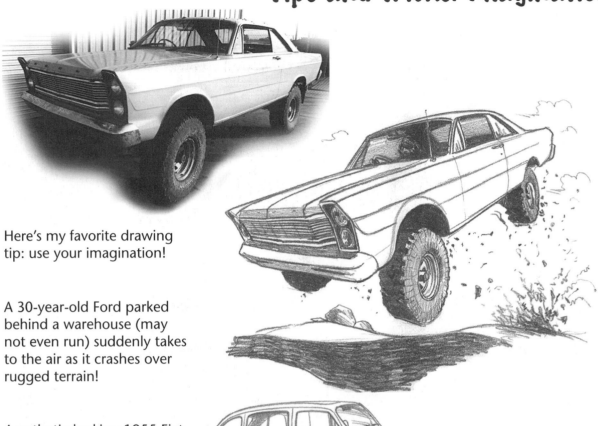

Here's my favorite drawing tip: use your imagination!

A 30-year-old Ford parked behind a warehouse (may not even run) suddenly takes to the air as it crashes over rugged terrain!

A pathetic-looking 1955 Fiat becomes a Lamborghini-stomping terror!

How about a cartoon based on a radio-controlled model?

Imagination: you've got it. Use it!

DO YOU LIKE THIS BOOK?

BE WISE...
CHECK OUT
THE WHOLE SET!

Draw Sports Figures
Draw Alien Fantasies
Draw Medieval Fantasies
Draw Rainforest Animals
Draw Desert Animals
Draw Grassland Animals
Draw Ocean Animals
Draw Insects
Draw Dinosaurs
Draw Cars
Draw 3-D
Learn To Draw Now!

DRAWING LESSONS
ONLINE...

...HOP OVER TO OUR
WEB SITE
WWW.DRAWBOOKS.COM